J 912 SHE

Shea, Therese

Reading map keys

S

4/15

S0-ARO-521

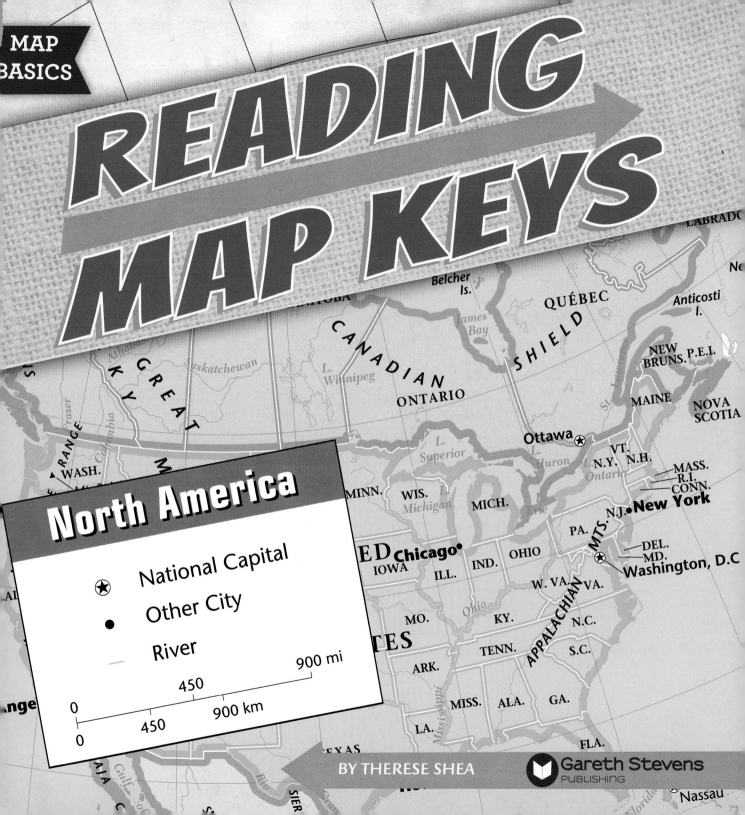

READING
MAP KEYS

North America

- ⊛ National Capital
- • Other City
- — River

900 mi
450
0
900 km
450
0

BY THERESE SHEA

Gareth Stevens
PUBLISHING

Please visit our website, www.garethstevens.com. For a free color catalog of all our high-quality books, call toll free 1-800-542-2595 or fax 1-877-542-2596.

Library of Congress Cataloging-in-Publication Data

Shea, Therese.
Reading map keys / by Therese Shea.
 p. cm. — (Map basics)
Includes index.
ISBN 978-1-4824-1074-7 (pbk.)
ISBN 978-1-4824-1075-4 (6-pack)
ISBN 978-1-4824-1073-0 (library binding)
1. Map reading — Juvenile literature. 2. Maps — Symbols — Juvenile literature. I. Shea, Therese. II. Title.
GA130.S52 2015
912.01—d23

First Edition

Published in 2015 by
Gareth Stevens Publishing
111 East 14th Street, Suite 349
New York, NY 10003

Copyright © 2015 Gareth Stevens Publishing

Designer: Sarah Liddell
Editor: Kristen Rajczak

Photo credits: Cover, p. 1 Globe Turner, LLC/Getty Images; p. 5 Globe Turner/Shutterstock.com;
p. 7 Dsdugan/Wikimedia Commons; p. 9 (map) Stacey Lynn Payne/Shutterstock.com; p. 9 (Interstate
90 shield) Ltljltlj/Wikimedia Commons; p. 11 amorfati.art/Shutterstock.com; p. 13 tele52/
Shutterstock.com; p. 15 Quibik/Wikimedia Commons; p. 17 Agrus/Shutterstock.com; p. 19 ekler/
Shutterstock.com; p. 21 (neighborhood) karamysh/Shutterstock.com; p. 21 (bus) Dan Kosmayer/
Shutterstock.com; p. 21 (school) MaxyM/Shutterstock.com.

All rights reserved. No part of this book may be reproduced in any form without
permission in writing from the publisher, except by a reviewer.

Printed in the United States of America

CPSIA compliance information: Batch #CS15GS: For further information contact Gareth Stevens, New York, New York at 1-800-542-2595.

CONTENTS

Words in the glossary appear in **bold** type the first time they are used in the text.

THE RIGHT KEY

Have you ever used the wrong key in a door? It probably didn't fit, and it certainly didn't let you open the door to get inside. Some maps use keys, too. Without the key, you might not be able to get where you want to go or even understand the **information** the map is presenting.

Because maps show large areas, they use **symbols**, pictures, and colors to **represent** places, landforms, and other features. A map key explains what these symbols mean.

JUST THE FACTS

A key may also be called a legend.

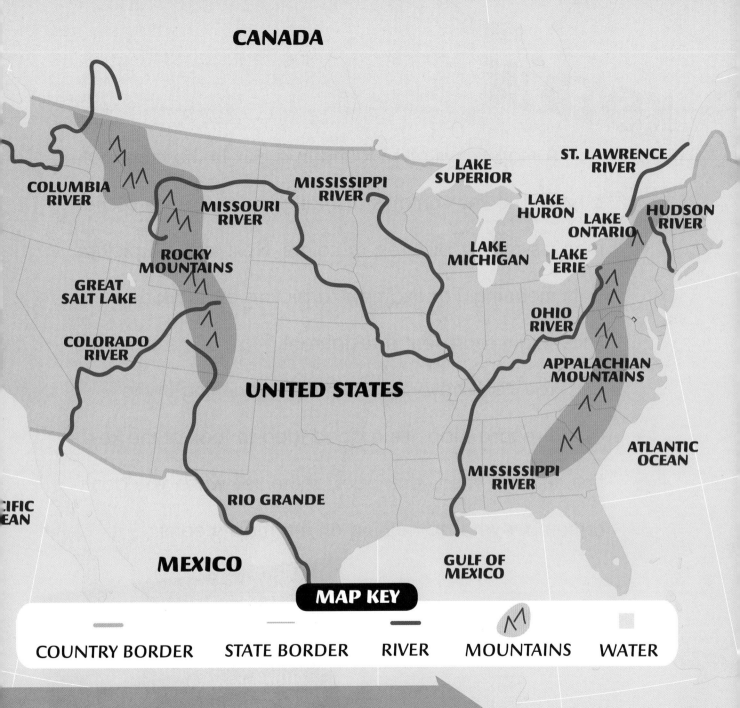

CANADA

COLUMBIA RIVER

MISSOURI RIVER

MISSISSIPPI RIVER

LAKE SUPERIOR

ST. LAWRENCE RIVER

LAKE HURON

LAKE ONTARIO

HUDSON RIVER

LAKE MICHIGAN

LAKE ERIE

ROCKY MOUNTAINS

GREAT SALT LAKE

COLORADO RIVER

UNITED STATES

OHIO RIVER

APPALACHIAN MOUNTAINS

ATLANTIC OCEAN

MISSISSIPPI RIVER

RIO GRANDE

PACIFIC OCEAN

MEXICO

GULF OF MEXICO

MAP KEY

COUNTRY BORDER · STATE BORDER · RIVER · MOUNTAINS · WATER

If a map didn't use symbols to represent things, it would have to be very, very large!

5

KEYED IN

A map key is often found in a box in the corner of a map. The key contains a small picture of each of the map's symbols, pictures, or colors. Next to each picture is its meaning. For example, a picture of a fork and knife might represent a restaurant.

You don't have to remember everything in the key to read a map. It's a good idea to look at the key first, though. Then, look back at the key when you don't remember what something on the map means.

JUST THE FACTS

Not all maps use the same symbols. In fact, many symbols used for US maps mean something else on maps made in other countries.

ST. JOE National Forest

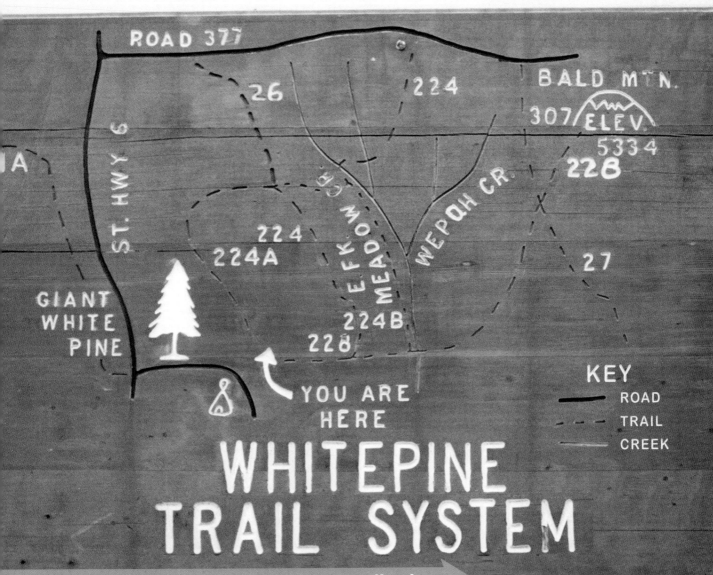

ROAD 377

26

224

BALD MTN.

307/ELEV.

5334

228

ST. HWY 6

EFKOM MEADOW CR.

WEPAH CR.

224
224A

224B

228

27

GIANT
WHITE
PINE

YOU ARE
HERE

KEY

ROAD
TRAIL
CREEK

WHITEPINE TRAIL SYSTEM

The key for this map of a national forest tells what
the different lines on the map mean. The blue lines,
for example, represent the creek.

If you want to know how to drive somewhere, you'll need more than a car key. Road maps, or street maps, can help you get there. A road map's key can tell you what kind of **route** to travel.

In the United States, most map keys show an **interstate** road as a red, white, and blue shield. National highways are black and white shields, and round signs are state highways. Each has a number instead of a name like a street has.

JUST THE FACTS

Interstate 90 is the longest US interstate highway. You could follow it from Washington State to Massachusetts.

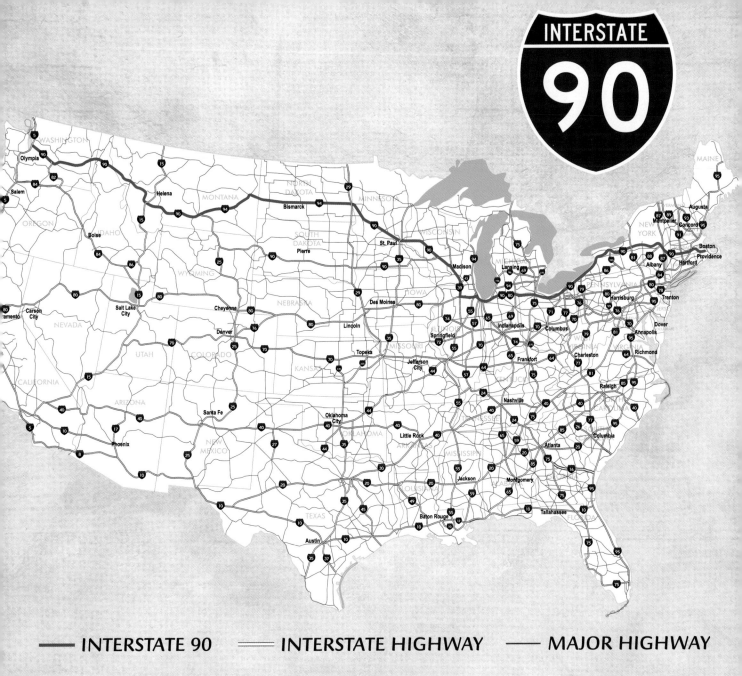

INTERSTATE 90

INTERSTATE 90 === **INTERSTATE HIGHWAY** — **MAJOR HIGHWAY**

You can follow a route on a map with your finger to see if it goes to the place you want to go.

CONFUSING COLORS

Physical maps tell you about the physical features of an area, such as mountains, valleys, and lakes. Water is usually blue, but you need to use the map key to figure out what other colors stand for.

This physical map of New York shows elevation, or height above sea level. The areas close to sea level are dark tan. White areas are the highest elevations. The Adirondack Mountains are in the northeast part of the state. Can you spot them using the key?

▲ MOUNT MARCY

HEIGHT ABOVE SEA LEVEL

- 3,000–5,500 ft.
- 1,800–3,000 ft.
- 1,200–1,800 ft.
- 600–1,200 ft.
- 300–600 ft.
- 150–300 ft.
- 0–150 ft.

New York's highest point is Mount Marcy in the Adirondack Mountains. It's 5,344 feet (1,629 m) tall.

11

LINES, STARS, AND DOTS

Political maps show man-made borders between states, countries, and other kinds of territories. For example, state and national borders are usually shown with a solid or dotted line. Sometimes both are used, so it's important to examine a political map's key.

Most political maps show state or country capitals, too. Often a star is used, but some maps use different symbols. Dots may stand for other major cities. When there's a key, there's no need to guess what each symbol means.

JUST THE FACTS
Many maps and globes are a combination of political and physical maps.

UNITED KINGDOM

BELGIUM

Calais

Lille

NORD-PAS-DE-CALAIS

Arras

Amiens

PICARDIE

LUX.

Charlesville

GERMANY

UPPER NORMANDY

Le Havre

Beauvais

Laon

Metz

Saint Lo

Rouen

Paris

Charlsons-sur-Marne

Bar-Le-Duc

ALSACE

Caen

Evreux

Versailles

CHAMPAGNE ARDENNE

Nancy

Strasbourg

Saint-Brieuc

LOWER NORMANDY

ILE-DE-FRANCE

LORRAINE

BRITTANY

Alencon

Evry

Troyes

Chaumont

Epinal

Colman

Quimper

Laval

Chartres

Melun

Vesoul

st

Rennes

Le Mans

Orleans

Auxerre

Belfort

Vannes

PAYS DE LA LOIRE

Blois

Dijon

Besancon

AUSTRIA

Angers

Tours

Bourges

BURGUNDY

FRANCHE COMTE

SWITZERLAND

St. Nazaire

Nantes

CENTRE

Nevers

Lons-Le-Saunier

Poitiers

Chateauroux

Moulins

Macon

La Rochelle

Gueret

Bourg-en-Bresse

POITOU CHARENTES

LIMOUSIN

Clermont-Ferrand

Lyon

Annecy

Angouleme

Limoges

AUVERGNE

Saint Etienne

RHONE ALPES

Grenoble

ITALY

Tulle

Le Puy

Bordeaux

Aurillac

Valence

AQUITAINE

Cahors

Mende

Privas

Gap

Agen

Rodez

Digne

Mont-de-Marsan

Auch

Nimes

Avignon

Bayonne

MIDI-PYRENEES

Albi

Montpellier

PROVENCE-ALPES-COTE D'AZUR

Cannes

Pau

Montauban

Toulouse

Tarbes

Carcassonne

Marseille

Toulon

Foix

LANGUEDOC-ROUSSILLON

Bastia

Perpignan

CORSICA

SPAIN

Ajaccio

National Capital — International Boundary
Region Capital — Regional Boundary
Other City
50 km
50 miles

This map of France shows how the country is divided into regions, or areas, and many major cities. Use the key to find France's national capital, Paris.

13

Many population maps use different colors to show how many people live in an area. The key explains what each color means. Without the key, the map would just look like someone colored it in messily!

The map on the next page shows the population per square kilometer (0.39 sq mi) of each country in the world. The key shows that a darker brown means more people live there. Lighter colors mean fewer people live in an area.

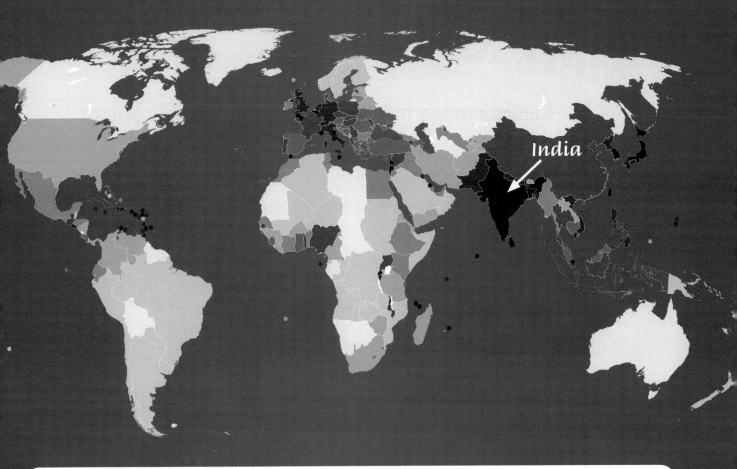

POPULATION (PEOPLE PER SQUARE KILOMETER)

0–10	
10–25	
25–50	
50–75	
75–100	
100–150	
150–300	
300–1000	
1000+	

On this map, India is a dark brown color. According to the map key, that means there are 300 to 1,000 people per square kilometer in the country.

Climate maps give facts about long-term weather conditions. These maps often use colors to represent conditions, so a key is necessary to find out what the colors mean.

Look at this map of South America. According to its key, parts colored reddish brown have a tropical climate, which means they're hot. Dark green represents the temperate climate areas, which have milder temperatures. The light green shows the parts of South America that are arid, or dry.

JUST THE FACTS

Climate maps from different time periods can show how **climate change** is affecting the planet.

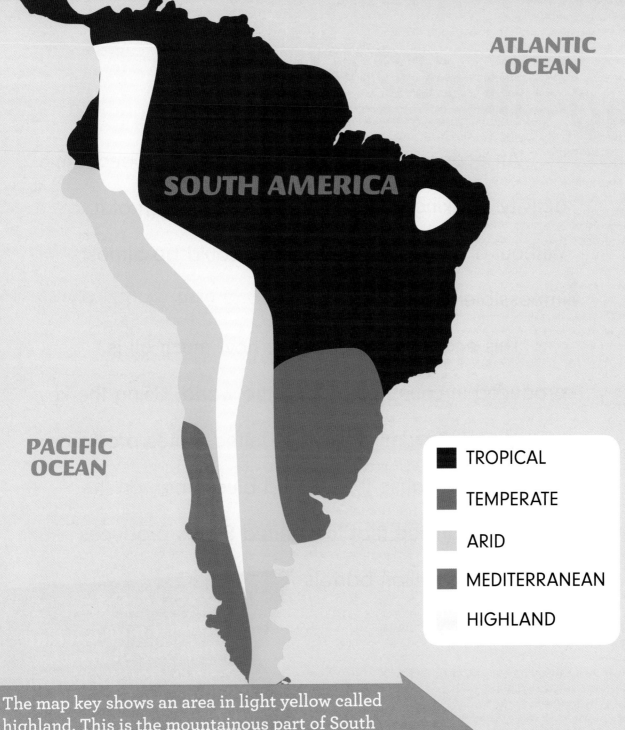

ATLANTIC
OCEAN

SOUTH AMERICA

PACIFIC
OCEAN

TROPICAL

TEMPERATE

ARID

MEDITERRANEAN

HIGHLAND

The map key shows an area in light yellow called
highland. This is the mountainous part of South
America, and it's commonly cooler than the
climate in the areas below and around it.

An **economic** map can show where an economic activity is taking place as well as how much of it. Without a key, an economic map could be almost impossible to read.

This economic map shows how much oil is produced in countries around the world. Using the key, can you tell how much oil the United States produces each day? Because it's colored blue-green on the map, you can see that the United States produces more than 1 million barrels of oil per day.

JUST THE FACTS

A **resource** map is a kind of map that shows where resources, usually natural resources, are located. Each resource is represented in the map's key.

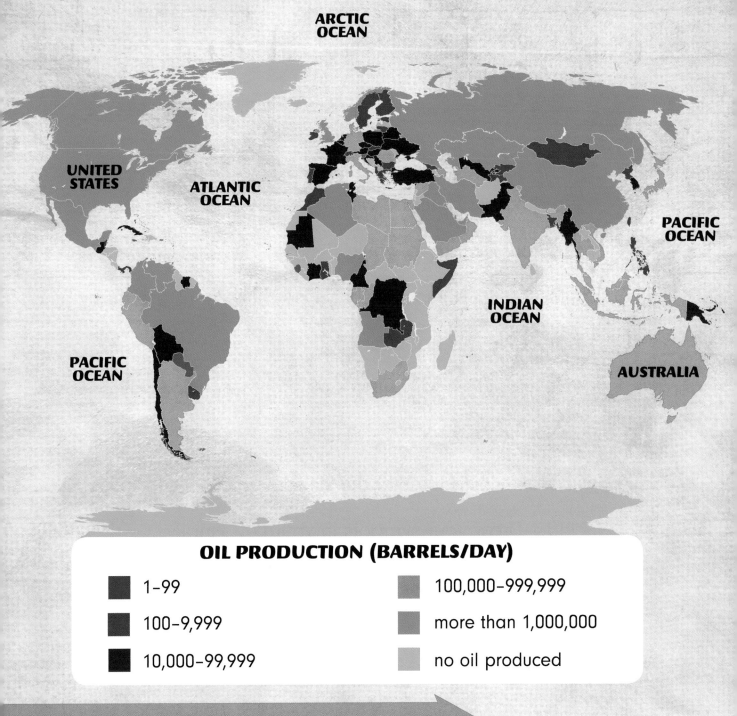

ARCTIC OCEAN

UNITED STATES

ATLANTIC OCEAN

PACIFIC OCEAN

PACIFIC OCEAN

INDIAN OCEAN

AUSTRALIA

OIL PRODUCTION (BARRELS/DAY)

- 1–99
- 100–9,999
- 10,000–99,999
- 100,000–999,999
- more than 1,000,000
- no oil produced

Use the key to find out how much oil Australia produces each day.

MAKE YOUR OWN MAP!

Maps and their keys can unlock many questions people have about the world. If you were going to make your own map, you'd first decide what you would be interested in showing other people. There are many examples in this book, but you might want to make a different kind of map—like a treasure map or a map of your neighborhood.

Next, you'd think of the symbols you'd need to include. Draw your symbols in your key. Finally, draw your map and place the key's symbols in the correct locations.

MAKE A MARVELOUS MAP!

MAP IDEA:
YOUR NEIGHBORHOOD

MAP IDEA:
YOUR ROUTE TO SCHOOL

MAP IDEA:
YOUR SCHOOL

KEY IDEAS:
HOUSES
ROADS
STORES
PARKS

KEY IDEAS:
HOUSES
ROAD CROSSINGS
BUS STOPS
SCHOOL

KEY IDEAS:
CLASSROOM
CAFETERIA
GYM
PRINCIPAL'S OFFICE

21

GLOSSARY

climate: the average weather conditions of a place over a period of time

climate change: long-term change in Earth's climate, caused partly by human activities such as burning oil and natural gas

economic: having to do with the production and use of goods and services

information: facts and knowledge

interstate: describing a road that forms part of the national system of highways connecting the major cities of the United States

represent: to stand for

resource: something in nature that can be used by people

route: a path that people travel

symbol: a picture or shape that stands for something else

BOOKS

Olien, Rebecca. *Map Keys.* New York, NY: Children's Press, 2013.

Shireman, Myrl, et. al. *Map Reading Skills.* Greensboro, NC: Mark Twain Media, 2012.

Waldron, Melanie. *How to Read a Map.* Chicago, IL: Capstone Raintree, 2013.

WEBSITES

Map Key: What Is It?
web.utk.edu/~rkirkla1/mapskills/mapkey_what.html
Read more about keys and other common parts of maps.

Mapping
education.nationalgeographic.com/education/mapping/kd/?ar_a=3equatorprimemeridian.htm
Play games, color, and learn more about different kinds of maps.

Publisher's note to educators and parents: Our editors have carefully reviewed these websites to ensure that they are suitable for students. Many websites change frequently, however, and we cannot guarantee that a site's future contents will continue to meet our high standards of quality and educational value. Be advised that students should be closely supervised whenever they access the Internet.

INDEX